Cat Stats

American Shorthairs

NICKI CLAUSEN-GRACE

BLACK
RABBIT
BOOKS

Bolt is published by Black Rabbit Books
P.O. Box 3263, Mankato, Minnesota, 56002.
www.blackrabbitbooks.com
Copyright © 2020 Black Rabbit Books

Jennifer Besel, editor; Catherine Cates,
interior designer; Grant Gould, cover designer;
Omay Ayres, photo researcher

Library of Congress Cataloging-in-Publication Data
Names: Clausen-Grace, Nicki, author.
Title: American shorthairs / by Nicki Clausen-Grace.
Description: Mankato, Minnesota : Black Rabbit Books, [2020] |
Series: Bolt. Cat stats | Audience: Age 8-12. | Audience: Grade 4 to 6. |
Includes bibliographical references and index.
Identifiers: LCCN 2018020570 (print) | LCCN 2018021826 (ebook) |
ISBN 9781680728040 (e-book) | ISBN 9781680727982 (library binding) |
ISBN 9781644660157 (paperback)
Subjects: LCSH: American shorthair cat—Juvenile literature.
Classification: LCC SF449.A45 (ebook) | LCC SF449.A45 C53 2020 (print) |
DDC 636.8/2—dc23
LC record available at https://lccn.loc.gov/2018020570

Printed in the United States of America. 1/19

Image Credits

Alamy: Quagga Media, 6;
iStock: Chalabala, 12–13; Dixi_, 28;
Viorika, 31; Volchanskiy, 1; Shutterstock:
Africa Studio, 23 (t), 24; alexavol, 8–9,
17 (br), 20–21 (kitten, adolescent & adult);
Astrid Gast, 25; Cat'chy Images, 20–21 (senior);
Chendongshan, 18 (t); CJansuebsri, 20–21 (bkgd
all circles); Elena Butinova, 17 (bl); HannaMonika,
17 (bc); Jean Andrian, 15; Kdonmuang, 26–27; Kirill
Vorobyev, 32; Renata Apanaviciene, 10 (b); Seregraff,
18 (b); SJ Allen, 4–5; TheRocky41, 17 (t); Vimvipa
Kosasaeng, Cover, 3; vvvita, 10 (t); WaitForLight,
14 (t); Yimmyphotography, 23 (b); tribalproduce.
com: tribalproduce, 14 (b)
Every effort has been made to contact
copyright holders for material reproduced
in this book. Any omissions will be
rectified in subsequent printings
if notice is given to
the publisher.

Contents

CHAPTER 1

Meet the

American Shorthair

A bird splashes playfully in a birdbath. It doesn't know it is being **stalked**. An American shorthair cat watches. Its hunting **instincts** make it want to pounce.

Shorthair cats that are not purebred are still called domestic shorthairs.

Working Cats

The American shorthair **breed** comes from European working cats. Those cats traveled on boats with early North American settlers. They even traveled with pilgrims on the *Mayflower*. The cats were known for catching rats.

In the 1800s, breeders began developing the shorthair cat. They called it the domestic shorthair. In 1966, the breed was renamed to American shorthair.

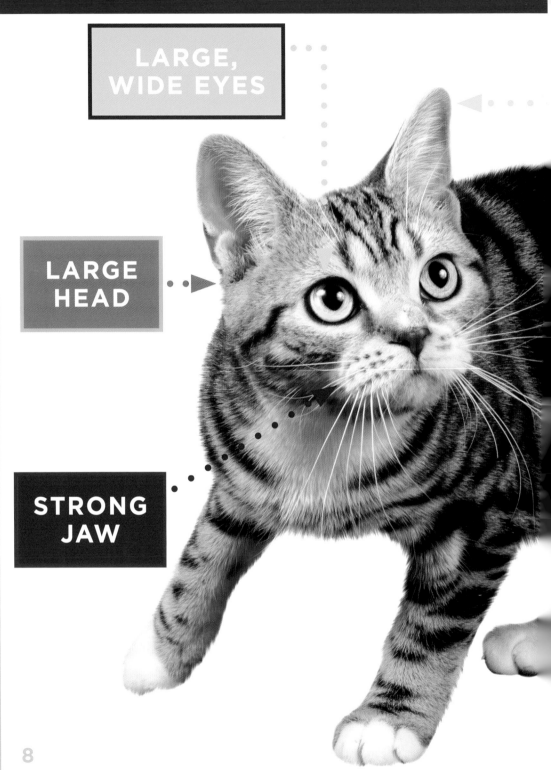

LARGE, WIDE EYES

LARGE HEAD

STRONG JAW

ROUNDED
EARS

THICK
TAIL

SHORT
COAT

9

CHAPTER 2

A Special

Personality

American shorthairs are easy to get along with. They like children, other cats, and nice dogs. They are friendly, but they don't need constant attention. Their favorite pastime is lying in a sunny spot watching for birds.

Hanging out with the Family

American shorthairs like the company of their families. But they don't always need to be held. They let their owners know when they want to cuddle. Sometimes just being nearby is what the cats like best.

Cat Games

chasing a toy on a string

getting treats from a puzzle toy

batting a ball

Playing Games

American shorthairs have strong
hunting instincts. But they don't need
to hunt rats anymore. Instead, these
cats like to play games. Puzzle toys are
a lot of fun. Games where the cat stalks
something is fun too.

CHAPTER 3

American Shorthairs'

American shorthairs are powerful. They are medium to large cats, weighing from 6 to 15 pounds (3 to 7 kilograms). Their legs are thick and strong. Their **muscular** bodies make them good hunters.

COMPARING SIZES

MAINE COON	RAGDOLL	AMERICAN SHORTHAIR

up to 25 POUNDS (11 kg)

up to 20 POUNDS

up to 15 POUNDS (7 kg)

Many Colors

American shorthairs have thick, shiny coats. They come in more than 80 different colors and patterns. The silver **tabby** is one of the most well known.

The cats' eyes come in many colors too. They can be blue, green, gold, or hazel.

Some shorthairs are odd-eyed. They have two different colored eyes.

American Shorthair

Life Cycle

Kittens learn to climb, run, and jump.

KITTEN

Older shorthairs move a little slower. These cats live more than 15 years.

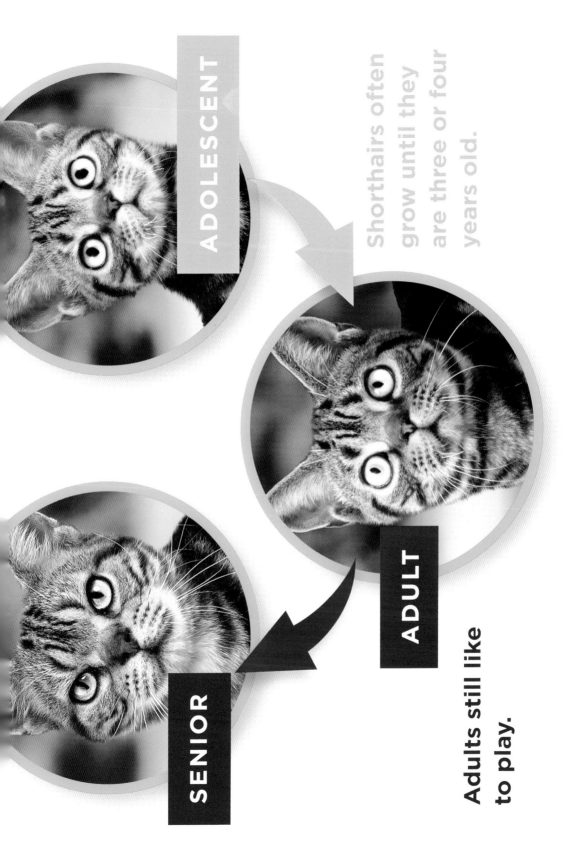

ADOLESCENT

Shorthairs often grow until they are three or four years old.

ADULT

Adults still like to play.

SENIOR

CHAPTER 4

Caring for American Shorthairs

American shorthairs are easy to **groom**. They need to be combed and have their teeth brushed weekly. It's good to trim their nails every two weeks. They also need food, water, and a clean litter box every day.

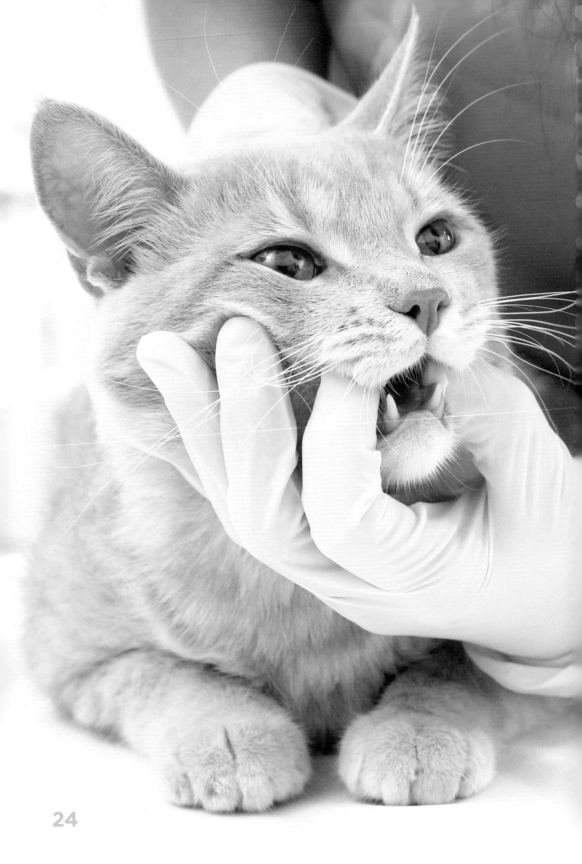

Health Concerns

American shorthairs are usually healthy. One problem to watch for is **obesity**. Owners must be careful to keep their shorthairs from overeating. Getting regular vet checkups can help avoid health problems.

Popular Pets

American shorthairs are popular pets. They are friendly and easy to live with. They enjoy company but don't need attention all the time. These are fun cats to be around.

Shorthairs will hunt insects or pests inside the house.

Is an American Shorthair

Answer the questions below. Then add up your points to see if a shorthair is a good fit.

1 **Do you want to spend a lot of time grooming your cat?**

A. Yes. I love brushing cats. **(1 point)**

B. I'd like to do it a few times a week. **(2 points)**

C. No. I like a cat that keeps itself clean. **(3 points)**

2 Do you want a cat that needs to be played with all the time?

A. I want to play cat games all day! **(1 point)**

B. I like to play most of the time. (2 points)

C. I'd like to play a little bit each day. **(3 points)**

3 Do you like cats with long, silky hair?

A. I love fluffy cats. **(1 point)**

B. I like long hair, but short hair is good too. (2 points)

C. I prefer a short, thick coat. **(3 points)**

. . . .

3 points
A shorthair is not your perfect match.
4–8 points
A shorthair might work.
But there might be a better breed for you.
9 points
You and a shorthair would get along well!

GLOSSARY

breed (BREED)—a particular kind of dog, cat, horse, or other animal

groom (GROOM)—to clean and care for someone or something

instinct (IN-stingkt)—a natural, unplanned behavior in response to something

muscular (MUS-kyu-lur)—having large and strong muscles

obesity (oh-BEE-si-tee)—the condition of being very fat or overweight

purebred (PYUR-brehd)—coming from members of a recognized breed, strain, or kind without mixing with other kinds over many generations

stalk (STALK)—to pursue prey in a sneaky way

tabby (TAH-bee)—a domestic cat with a striped and spotted coat

BOOKS

Furstinger, Nancy, and John Willis. *American Shorthair Cats.* All about Cats. New York: AV2 by Weigl, 2018.

Leaf, Christina. *American Shorthairs.* Cool Cats. Minneapolis: Bellwether Media, 2016.

Schuh, Mari. *American Shorthair Cats.* Favorite Cat Breeds. Mankato, MN: Amicus High Interest, Amicus Ink, 2017.

WEBSITES

American Shorthair
www.animalplanet.com/tv-shows/cats-101/videos/american-shorthair

Breed Profile: The American Shorthair
cfa.org/Breeds/BreedsAB/AmericanShorthair.aspx

The American Shorthair Cat
www.cat-breeds-encyclopedia.com/American-Shorthair-cat.html